# ON BREXIT

**MATTHEW PRITCHETT**

studied at St Martin's School of Art in
London and first saw himself published in
the *New Statesman* during one of its rare
lapses from high seriousness. He has been
the *Daily Telegraph*'s front-page pocket
cartoonist since 1988. In 1995, 1996, 1999,
2005, 2009 and 2013 he was the winner of
the Cartoon Arts Trust Award and in 1991,
2004 and 2006 he was 'What the Papers
Say' Cartoonist of the Year. In 1996, 1998,
2000, 2008, 2009 and 2018 he was the *UK
Press* Cartoonist of the Year and in 2015 he
was awarded the Journalists' Charity Award.
In 2002 he received an MBE.

Own your favourite Matt cartoons.
Browse the full range of Matt
cartoons and buy online at
www.telegraph.co.uk/mattprints
or call 0191 6030178.

**The Daily Telegraph**

ON BREXIT

ORION

An Orion Paperback

First published in Great Britain in 2019 by Orion Books
A division of the Orion Publishing Group Ltd
Carmelite House
50 Victoria Embankment
London
EC4Y 0DZ

A Hachette UK Company

10 9 8 7 6 5 4 3 2 1

A CIP catalogue record for this book is available from the British Library.

ISBN: 978 1 4091 9225 1

Printed and bound by CPI Group (UK) Ltd, Croydon, CR0 4YY

The Orion Publishing Group's policy is to use papers that are natural,
renewable and recyclable products and made from wood grown in
sustainable forests. The logging and manufacturing processes are expected
to conform to the environmental regulations of the country of origin.

www.orionbooks.co.uk

MATT

ON BREXIT

'I'm an EU genie, I grant you wishes that may be watered down or vetoed'

'Exquisitely crafted chocolates with mildly disappointing centres'

**Cameron's renegotiation with the EU begins**

**Cameron's renegotiation with the EU begins**

'I feel the wording of the question "Do you take this man ...?" is biased towards an "I do" outcome'

**Referendum wording row**

'We can't BLAME Europe if we're not IN Europe'

**The campaign begins...**

'We don't need to be part of a failing EU, we're big enough to fail on our own'

Sorry. While you were out we were able to deliver the Government's EU leaflet.

The campaign begins...

'I'm leaving you for someone on a rival leave Europe campaign'

'It's my new Telegraph T-shirt'

The campaign begins…

'If you insist on going out,
I don't want you nagging five
minutes later to be let back in'

'When you asked whether
I'm an "Innie" or "Outie" were
you talking about Europe or
belly buttons?'

**The campaign begins…**

**Project Fear starts**

'I can't divulge my sources,
but I happen to know
the Queen hates poodles'

'The PM said if you
could hit Boris it
would be appreciated'

**The Queen's dragged into it**

'At the last election he was a
Shy Tory and now he's a
Bashful Leaver'

'GET IT BACK!
I've changed my mind again'

**The Nation Decides**

'Let's never ask the public for their views ever again'

**Leave wins**

'I'm studying politics. The course covers the period from 8am on Thursday to lunchtime on Friday'

**Cameron resigns. Leadership contest. Labour against Corbyn.**

'My father fought in the
Tory leadership election.
He never speaks of the
things he saw'

'We need migrants to do the
jobs Brits won't or can't do.
Like Prime Minister or
Leader of the Opposition'

**All parties in disarray**

**All parties in disarray**

**Early days of Brexit**

'I favour a hard Xmas. No sending money, no trading gifts and definitely no free movement of relatives'

'Will I be home before the UK has left the EU?'

**Early days of Brexit**

'This Brexit is too hard and this one is too soft'

'Two Englishmen in Whitehall. One says "Which way to Brexit?" The other one replies "I wouldn't start from here"'

**Early days of Brexit**

'They swarm in, claim expenses and take all the country's claret'

'I seem to remember my family motto is "Thwart the Will of the People"'

**Article 50 meets opposition**

'If the UK is destroyed in a nuclear attack, these are the codes for triggering Article 50'

'I wish Putin would hack into the UK's Brexit plans and tell us what's going on'

**Ongoing confusion**

'Thank goodness we moved here after the Brexit vote. Civilisation will have collapsed by now'

**The fall-out**

'Prize money is £2m or a punnet of strawberries, whichever is worth more in two weeks time'

**The pound falls**

**House prices fall**

**Marmite becomes more expensive**

'And England scored
458 runs, despite Brexit'

**But there was some good news**

'The polls are narrowing.
Now is the time for
strong, stable panicking'

**May calls snap election**

'My dad's an opinion pollster, I hope he never loses that sense of wonder and surprise at election results'

'It turns out the voters are bloody difficult as well'

**Election doesn't go to plan**

'That's not the Queen. That's how the DUP travel these days'

'I'd just turned to my wife and said "Finally, we're taking back control"'

**Working majority costs £1billion**

**May back in Brussels**

**May back in Brussels**

'Prime Minister, the Brexit bill is €100bn and the EU wants to know if you'd like to add a tip'

'The European Court of Justice demanded to rule on all line calls'

**More fall-out**

'Here is your lovely blue passport. That will be four shillings and thruppence'

**But blue passports return**

'Distinguishing features: absolutely livid'

**...they'll be made in France**

'They can deliver our new
passports when they
come here to catch our fish'

'To be frank, this was
one of my red lines'

**Fishing row**

'Ice cream? No, this is
Philip Hammond's
ministerial car'

'While we work on our Brexit
forecast, this man will play
some very sad music'

**Hammond accused of being a Remoaner**

'I must warn you, in the
event of a no-deal Brexit
there will have to be an
emergency Hallowe'en'

'It's the Bank of England's
Christmas jumper'

**Doom and gloom**

'One is suddenly struck by a sense of how insignificant the British are'

'Should we let Mrs May inside to make her speech?'

**EU freezing us out**

'I say we send a moped gang to Brussels to negotiate Brexit. They wouldn't stand for any nonsense'

'Thank you for calling the EU. Unfortunately nobody is available to reject your customs plan. Your call is not important to us'

**Endless negotiations**

**Endless negotiations**

**Immigration**

'If we get to the UK, we can
all live in a van outside
Alan Bennett's house'

'Ready? The first to 21 points
gets into the country'

**Immigration**

**Immigration**

**World Cup starts**

'I don't want to alarm you,
but at any moment
Liam Fox could arrive
and ask for a trade deal'

'We're from the UK.
We've come to sell you
Cornish pasties and
bagless vacuum cleaners'

**Trade deals anyone?**

**Cabinet meet to see deal**

**Irish backstop revealed**

**Irish border**

'I should have written it down. While I was lying awake in the heat I solved the Irish border question'

'It's not for the royal baby. I'm knitting a soft Irish border'

Irish border

**Brexit getting softer?**

'I hope Mrs May keeps the receipt for this Brexit. We might want to exchange it for a different one'

'Is this the secret plot against Jeremy Corbyn, or the secret plot against Theresa May?'

**May's deal causes resignations**

'I'm on the Brexit diet. I fast
on days when Labour back
Brexit, and eat normally on
days when they oppose it'

'I used to be a Labour
whip, so herding cats
is a piece of cake'

**Labour has its own problems**

'Letters on parchment, catchy lute music and a Latin dictionary. We've found Rees-Mogg's leadership campaign HQ'

**Moves against May**

'It causes more rows than Monopoly, and lasts longer than a 1,000 piece jigsaw'

**Fall-out continues**

'Our roof voted to leave.
Stop remoaning'

'I'd like to join the Euro
army. There's a Brexit deal
I'm trying to forget'

**Fall-out continues**

**No deal worries**

'And in here they're preparing for a no-deal Brexit'

'In a major concession, Mrs May offered to take no deal off the table and put it on the sideboard'

**No deal worries**

'This refers to the number of
Mars bars the UK will have
after a no-deal Brexit'

'I'm stockpiling myrrh
in case there's a
no-deal Brexit'

**No deal worries**

'Uh-oh'

**Mad cow disease returns**

'When my hamster is in heaven will it meet the Chequers plan?'

**Chequers deal remains unpopular**

'Prime Minister, NASA has discovered living beings on Mars and they're all against your Brexit plan'

**Mrs May's deal remains unpopular**

**Withdrawal deal**

**Disappointment sets in**

'Why don't the BBC film crews in Westminster step in to stop this Brexit tragedy?'

**Attenborough film crew save penguin**

'A good guide to what happens next is to ask yourself how this could get any worse'

**And Brexit rumbles on**

'After Brexit I don't want EU boats coming into British waters and catching all our plastic'

'You may need to pour yourself a stiff drink before I begin'

**Brexit rumbles on**

'It's so pure and lovely at first and then it turns into a slushy mess'

'It's my Brexit dividend hat'

**Brexit rumbles on**

'Let in any highly-skilled
migrants. Particularly
if they have a Brexit plan'

'I'm thinking of giving this up
to campaign for orderly,
competent government'

**Brexit rumbles on**

'We're desperate for a second referendum. We sent our Romanian cleaners on the People's Vote march'

**Brexit rumbles on**

'If we can't work out how to leave, no cheese becomes a very real possibility'

'We've left out a glass of whisky and a carrot for Mrs May. That's all she'll get'

**May heads back to Brussels**

**May heads back to Brussels**

'Remember, whatever happens, Mrs May is always having a worse day'

'Is there anywhere in the world that isn't laughing at the British right now?'

**May heads back to Brussels**

**No one knows what they want**

'Well, that went better than I was expecting'

'Bad news, we're closing. We can't compete with the House of Commons'

May loses meaningful vote by 230

'Of course, you know what this means, don't you? No, neither do I'

May loses meaningful vote by 230

'Whitehall? Go past the
"Nazi Scum" chants, then
straight on till you get to
shouts of "Fascist Liar"'

**Public gets angrier**

'We solved the mystery. That
whining sound is coming
from Government ministers'

**Business fall-out**

'I voted Leave to stop the free movement of vacuum cleaners'

'Your Vauxhall is now French. Will it be allowed to stay in the UK after Brexit?'

**Business fall-out**

'This way Mrs May won't
even have to land'

'And now, once again,
it's Ode to Joy'

**May to Brussels (again)**

**Tusk's unfortunate comment**

'We need a Plan B. I don't mind compromising – but not with people I disagree with'

'We're not moving the date of Brexit, but we might add an extra 90 days to February'

**Deadline looms**

'MPs' holidays have been cancelled. That tin can won't kick itself down the road'

'Geoffrey Cox is negotiating in Brussels. The EU has sent us a ransom note and part of his ear'

**The final countdown . . .**

**Brexit**
Soft & very long

CRUFTS 2019

'Now remove the Irish
backstop from the
Withdrawal Agreement'

'The meaingful vote is on March 12. I'm not sure the Labour and Tory parties will still exist by then'

'Forget the Ides of March, the 12th is going to be a complete s***show'

**Meaningful Vote 2**

'It has just been revealed that the past two and a half years have all been a bad dream that David Cameron was having'

'If Mrs May has taught us anything, it's that persevering isn't always such a good idea'

**Meaningful Vote 2**

'When books are written about this, remind me not to read any of them'

'To get the title of your own Brexit plan, it's the name of your first pet, followed by your street and then the word "compromise" '

**Meaningful Vote 2**

'WAIT! I want to ask
you for a third time!'

'I'm going for a third,
and maybe a fourth,
Meaningful Drink'

**Meaningful Vote 3**

'Future generations will not forgive us if they have to study this in history lessons'

'What bad luck for Mrs May. This week would have gone so much better if she hadn't got her voice back'

**Meaningful Vote 3**

'The Prime Minister asked for a coffee. I said only if she set a date for her departure'

'If Mrs May promises to leave Number 10 soon, how can we be sure she'll pull it off?'

**May bargains with MPs**

'What do we want least?
When don't we want it?'

'If this ginger biscuit is a hard
Brexit, and this cup of tea
is the House of Commons ...'

**MPs debate alternatives**

'Nothing has changed'

'I booked a table with you at 8pm on the 29th March to celebrate Brexit. We might be a bit late …'

**And we're . . . still in**